Nothing Solemn

D1580517

A typing cockroach? A singing
cow? Absurd, of course, but in
a book that promises you
Nothing Solemn you must expect
such a riot of comical creatures
and hilarious happenings as
you will find in the pages that
follow.

Cover illustration by Graham Round

Nothing Solemn

An anthology of comic verse
compiled by Kenneth Agar

Illustrated by Graham Round

Evans Brothers Limited London

Published by Evans Brothers Limited
Montague House, Russell Square,
London, W.C.1.

© Evans Brothers Limited 1973

First published 1973

Set in Monotype 11 on 14pt Imprint and
printed in Great Britain by
Cox & Wyman Ltd, London, Reading and
Fakenham

CSD ISBN 237 0 44680 4 PRA 3446
PB ISBN 0 237 44683 9

Contents

Tall, and Sometimes Ridiculous Tales

Sheer Nonsense

Some Odds and Ends to End With

You Ought To Know

There was once a book called
NOTHING SERIOUS,
Which, nevertheless
Grew rather lonely,
And wanted a friend –
Somebody not too serious,
Not too grave,
Not too solemn,
But rather like itself –
And it *did* rather like itself,
Not taking itself
Too seriously.
So,
It chose this book
Because it felt that there's
Nothing Seriously Wrong
About a book
That contains
NOTHING SOLEMN!

Creatures...Strange and Rare

The Porcupine

Any hound a porcupine nudges
Can't be blamed for harbouring grudges.
I know one hound that laughed all winter
At a porcupine that sat on a splinter.

Ogden Nash

The Serpent

There was a Serpent who had to sing.
There was. There was.
He simply gave us Serpenting.
Because. Because.
He didn't like his Kind of Life;
He couldn't find a proper Wife;
He was a Serpent with a soul;
He got no Pleasure down his Hole.
And so, of course, he had to Sing,
And Sing he did, like Anything!
The Birds, they were, they were Astounded;
And various Measures Propounded
To stop the Serpent's Awful Racket:
They bought a Drum. He wouldn't Whack it.
They sent – you always send – to Cuba
And got a Most Commodious Tuba;
They got a Horn, they got a Flute,
But Nothing would suit.

He said, 'Look, Birds, all this is futile:
I do *not* like to Bang or Tootle.'
And then he cut loose with a Horrible Note
That practically split the Top of his Throat.
'You see,' he said, with a Serpent's Leer,
'I'm Serious about my Singing Career!'
And the Woods Resounded with many a Shriek
As the Birds flew off to the End of Next Week.

Theodore Roethke

Some Natural History

the patagonian
penguin
is a most
peculiar
bird
he lives on
pussy
willows
and his tongue
is always furred
the porcupine
of chile
sleeps his life away
and that is how
the needles
get into the hay
the argentinian
oyster
is a very
subtle gink

for when he's being eaten
he pretends he is
a skink
when you see
a sea gull
sitting
on a bald man's dome
she likely thinks
she's nesting
on her rocky
island home
do not tease
the inmates
when strolling
through the zoo
for they have
their finer feelings
the same
as me and you
oh deride not
the camel

if grief should
make him die
his ghost will come
to haunt you
with tears
in either eye
and the spirit of
a camel
in the midnight gloom
can be so very
cheerless
as it wanders
round the room

Don Marquis

That Cat

The cat that comes to my window sill
When the moon looks cold and the night is still –
He comes in a frenzied state alone
With a tail that stands like a pine tree cone,
And says: 'I have finished my evening lark,
And I think I can hear a hound dog bark.
My whiskers are froze 'nd stuck to my chin.
I do wish you'd git up and let me in.'
       That cat gits in.

But if in the solitude of the night
He doesn't appear to be feeling right,
And rises and stretches and seeks the floor,
And some remote corner he would explore,
And doesn't feel satisfied just because
There's no good spot for to sharpen his claws,
And meows and canters uneasy about
Beyond the least shadow of any doubt
       That cat gits out.

Ben King

The Kitty-Cat Bird

The Kitty-Cat Bird, he sat on a Fence.
Said the Wren, your Song isn't worth 10 cents.
You're a Fake, you're a Fraud, you're a Hor-rid Pretense!
– Said the Wren to the Kitty-Cat Bird.

You've too many Tunes, and none of them Good;
I wish you would act like a bird really should,
Or stay by yourself down deep in the wood,
– Said the Wren to the Kitty-Cat Bird.

You mew like a Cat, you grate like a Jay:
You squeak like a Mouse that's lost in the Hay,
I wouldn't be You for even a day,
– Said the Wren to the Kitty-Cat Bird.

The Kitty-Cat Bird, he moped and he cried.
Then a real cat came with a Mouth so Wide,
That the Kitty-Cat Bird just hopped inside;
At last I'm myself! – and he up and died
– Did the Kitty – the Kitty-Cat Bird.

You'd better not laugh; and don't say, 'Pooh!'
Until you have thought this Sad Tale through:
Be sure that whatever you are is you
– Or you'll end like the Kitty-Cat Bird.

Theodore Roethke

The National Health Cow

I strolled into a farmyard
When no one was about
Treading past the troubles
I raised my head to shout.

'Come out the Cow with glasses,'
I called and rolled my eye,
It ambled up toward me;
I milked it with a sigh.

'You're just in time,' the cow said,
Its eyes were all aglaze,
'I'm feeling like an elephant,
I aren't been milked for days.'

'Why is this?' I asked it,
Tugging at its throttles.
'I don't know why, perhaps it's 'cause
MY milk comes out in bottles.'

'That's handy for the government,'
I thought, and in a tick
The cow fell dead all sudden
(*I'd smashed it with a brick.*)

John Lennon

The Hippopotamus's Birthday

He has opened all his parcels
    but the largest and the last;
His hopes are at their highest
    and his heart is beating fast.
O happy Hippopotamus,
    what lovely gift is here?
He cuts the string. The world stands still.
    A pair of boots appear!

O little Hippopotamus,
    the sorrows of the small!
He dropped two tears to mingle
    with the flowing Senegal;
And the 'Thank you' that he uttered
    was the saddest ever heard
In the Senegambian jungle
    from the mouth of beast or bird.

E. V. Rieu

The Flattered Flying Fish

Said the Shark to the Flying Fish over the phone:
'Will you join me tonight? I am dining alone.
Let me order a nice little dinner for two!
And come as you are, in your shimmering blue.'

Said the Flying Fish: 'Fancy remembering me,
And the dress that I wore at the Porpoises' tea!'
'How could I forget?' said the Shark in his guile:
'I expect you at eight!' and rang off with a smile.

She has powdered her nose; she has put on her things;
She is off with one flap of her luminous wings.
O little one, lovely, light-hearted and vain,
The Moon will not shine on your beauty again!

E. V. Rieu

After a Visit to the Natural History Museum

This is the Wiggledywastious,
Very remarkable beast.
Nose to tail an eighth of a mile;
Took him an acre or two to smile;
Took him a quarter 'f an hour to wink;
Swallowed a pond for his morning drink.
Oh! Would it had been vouchsafed to us
Upon the Wiggledywastious
Our wondering eyes to feast!

This is the Ptoodlecumtumpsydyl,
Rather unusual bird.
Had a mouth before and behind;
Ate whichever way he'd a mind;
Spoiled his digestion, so they say,
Pindled and dwindled quite away,
Or else he might have been living still,
The singular Ptoodlecumtumpsydyl.
A pity, upon my word!

This is the Ichthyosnortoryx,
Truly astonishing fish.
Used to snort in a terrible way;
Scared the lobsters to death they say;
Had a nose like a tea-kettle spout;
Broke it snorting, and so died out.
Sad! If he hadn't got into this fix,
We might have made of the 'Snortoryx
A very acceptable dish.

Laura Richards

Crocodile

Once there was a Crocodile
(Croc! Croc! Crocodile!),
A Crocodile of taste and style
And elegant attire;
He strolled down Piccadilly,
Singing carols in Swahili,
Wearing spats he'd bought in Chile,
And a-puffing at a briar . . .

Crocodile!
Crocodile!
Croc!
Croc!
Crocodile!
Alexander Crocodile, Esquire.

He'd a hat from Mozambique,
He could chat in modern Greek . . .
But they crowded round and shouted:
'That's a silly way to speak!
What a funny sort of freak!
What a cheek!
Croco-Freak!
What a snout!
What a beak!

Hurdy-gurdy! How absurd!
What an ugly sort of bird!
Croco-freak!
Croco-freak!
Croco-freak!'

Schoolboys raced after him,
Sneering,
Insulting him;
Chimney-sweeps laughed at him,
Jeering
And pelting him;
Urchins cocked snooks at him,
Students chucked books at him,
Hungry old mongrels
Flung horrible looks at him . . .
Then a scruffy Pekinese
Bit his trousers at the knees
With ferocity!
(O, a scrubby little pup,
Unattractively brought up,
A disgusting little pup,
An atrocity!)

More in sorrow than in anger
Alexander spread his jaws,
And devoured the brash offender,
Collar,
Pedigree,
And paws!

Kornei Chukousky
translated by
Richard Coe

There is no more room for the rest of
this story, but it all ended happily . . .

Tall, and Sometimes Ridiculous Tales

The Magic Pudding

Ho, the cook of the *Saucy Sausage*,
Was a feller called Curry and Rice,
A son of a gun as fat as a tun
With face as round as a hot-cross bun,
Or a barrel, to be precise.

One winter's morn we rounds the Horn,
A-rollin' homeward bound.
We strikes on the ice, goes down in a trice,
And all on board but Curry and Rice
And me an' Sam is drowned.

For Sam an' me an' the cook, yer see,
We climbs on a lump of ice,
And there in the sleet we suffered a treat
For several months from frozen feet,
With nothin' at all but ice to eat,
And ice does not suffice.

And Sam and me we couldn't agree
With the cook at any price.
We was both as thin as a piece of tin
While that there cook was busting his skin
On nothin' to eat but ice.

Says Sam to me, 'It's a mystery
More deep than words can utter;
Whatever we do, here's me an' you,
Us both as thin as Irish stoo,
While he's as fat as butter.'

But late one night we wakes in fright
To see by a pale blue flare,
That cook has got in a phantom pot
A big plum-duff an' a rump-steak hot,
And the guzzlin' wizard is eatin' the lot,
On top of the iceberg bare.

Now Sam an' me can never agree
What happened to Curry and Rice.
The whole affair is shrouded in doubt,
For the night was dark and the flare went out,
And all we heard was a startled shout,
Though I think meself, in the subsequent rout,
That us bein' thin, an' him bein' stout,
In the middle of pushin' an' shovin' about.
He – MUST HAVE FELL OFF THE ICE.

Norman Lindsay

A Cautionary Tale
Mr. Thomas Meddle Senior
Who Did

My tale begins with Junior Tom,
Who made his own Atomic Bomb:
He built it with a clockwork spring,
A photographic flashlight thing,
A detonator found at Chatham,
And a slightly bent Uranium Atom.
Alas! One day, with son at school,
His father, prowling round the tool
Shed in a bored and idle manner,
Straightened the Atom with a spanner!

Six miles away, in the dusty gloom
Of a dismal desk-encumbered room,
The boys abruptly ceased to think
Of Magna Carta, canes, and ink,
But ducked their tuppennies at the flash,
Felt all the building rock and crash,

Then, crawling from beneath the rubble,
Bewildered by the hubble-bubble,
And sitting up in startled crowd,
Beheld a monstrous mushroom cloud,
Fantastically broad and high,
Surge blackly up into the sky . . .

Said Junior Tom, 'How like the Pater!
Bang goes my only detonator!'

J. A. Lindon

The Lady and the Bear

A Lady came to a Bear by a Stream.
'O why are you fishing that way?
Tell me, dear Bear there by the Stream,
Why are you fishing that way?'

'I am what is known as a Biddly Bear –
That's why I'm fishing this way.
We Biddly's are Pee-culiar Bears.
And so – I'm fishing this way.

And besides, it seems there's a Law:
A most, most exactious Law
Says a Bear

Doesn't dare
Doesn't dare
Doesn't DARE

Use a Hook or a Line,
Or an old piece of Twine,
Not even the end of his Claw, Claw, Claw,
Not even the end of his claw.
Yes, a Bear has to fish with his Paw, Paw, Paw,
A Bear has to fish with his Paw.'

'O it's Wonderful how with a flick of your Wrist,
You can fish out a fish, out a fish, out a fish,
If *I* were a fish I just couldn't resist
You, when you are fishing that way, that way,
When you are fishing that way.'

And at that the Lady slipped from the Bank
And fell in the Stream still clutching a Plank,
But the Bear just sat there until she Sank;
As he went on fishing his way, his way,
As he went on fishing his way.

Theodore Roethke

A Dutchman's Dog Story

Dere vhas a leedle vomans once
　Who keept a leedle shtore,
Und had a leedle puppy dog
　Dot shtoodt pefore der door.
Und evfery dime der peoples coom
　He opened vide him's jaw.
　　Schnip! Schnap! shoost so,
　　　Und bite dem.

Vun day anoder puppy dog
　Coombs runnin' down der shtreet,
Oudt of Herr Schneider's sausage-shop,
　Vhere he had shtoled some meat;
Und after him der Schneider man –
　Der vhind vhas not more fleet.
　　Whir-r-r! Whist! shoost so,
　　　Like vinkin'!

Der leedle voman's puppy dog
    Vhas lookin' at der fun,
Her barkit at der Schneider man,
    Und right pefore him run;
Den fell him down, dot Schneider man,
    Like shooted mit a gun.
        Bang! Crash! shoost so,
            Und voorser.

Der puppy dog dot shtoled der meat,
    Roon'd on und got avhay;
Der leedle voman's puppy dog
    Der Schneider man did slay,
Und make him indo sausages –
    Dot's vot der peoples say.
        Chip! Chop! shoost so,
            Und sell him.

Der Moral

Der moral is, don't inderfere
　　Vhen droubles is aroundt;
Der man dot's in der fightin' crowd
　　Vhill get hurt I'll be pound.
Mind your own peesness, dot is pest,
　　In life she vhill be found
　　　　Yaw! Yaw! shoost so,
　　　　　　I pet you.

J. T. Brown

The Red Herring

There was once a high wall, a bare wall. And
against this wall, there was a ladder,
a long ladder. And on the ground,
under the ladder, there was a red
herring. A dry red herring.

And then a man came along. And in his hands
(they were dirty hands) this man had
a heavy hammer, a long nail
(it was also a sharp nail) and
a ball of string. A thick ball of string.

All right. So the man climbed up
the ladder (right up to the top)
and knocked in the sharp nail:
spluk! Just like that.
Right on top of the wall. The bare wall.

Then he dropped the hammer. It dropped
right down to the ground. And onto the nail
he tied a piece of string, a long
piece of string, and onto the string
he tied the red herring. The dry red herring.

And let it drop. And then he climbed
down the ladder (right down
to the bottom), picked up the hammer
and also the ladder (which was pretty heavy)
and went off. A long way off.

And since then, that red herring, the dry
red herring on the end of the string, which is
quite a long piece, has been
very very slowly swinging and
swinging to a stop. A full stop.

I expect you wonder why I made
up this story, such a simple story. Well,
I did it just to annoy people.
Serious people. And perhaps also
to amuse children. Small children.

George Macbeth

Biby

A muvver was barfin' 'er biby one night,
The youngest of ten and a tiny young mite,
The muvver was poor and the biby was thin,
Only a skelington covered in skin;
The muvver turned rahnd for the soap orf the rack,
She was not a moment but when she turned back,
The biby was gorn; and in anguish she cried,
'Oh where is my biby?' – The angels replied:

'Your biby 'as fell dahn the plug-'ole,
Your biby 'as gorn dahn the plug;
The poor little thing was so skinny and thin
'E oughter been barfed in a jug;
Your biby is perfectly 'appy,
'E won't need a barf any more;
Your biby 'as fell dahn the plug-ole,
Not lorst, but gorn before!'

Anon.

Pussy Café

This is a story about Mehitabel, the cat. She cannot type, so her friend, Archy the Cockroach, does it for her. Archy writes without punctuation as he types by butting the keys of the typewriter with his head, and he is not able to reach the keys that make capital letters or punctuation marks.

for some weeks said
mehitabel the cat continuing the
story of her life i
lived in that barroom and
though the society was
not what i had been used to yet i
cannot say that it was
not interesting three
times a day in
addition to scraps from
the free lunch
and an occasional mouse
i was given a saucer

full of beer sometimes i
was given more and
when i was feeling
frolicsome it was the custom
for the patrons to gather
round and watch me
chase my tail until
i would suddenly fall
asleep at that time
they gave me the
nickname of pussy cafe but
one day i left the
place in the pocket
of a big fur
overcoat worn by
a gentleman who was
carrying so much that i thought

a little extra burden would
not be noticed he got
into a taxi cab
which soon afterwards
pulled up in front of
a swell residence up town
and wandered up the
steps well said his
wife meeting him in the
hallway you are here
at last but where is my
mother whom i sent you to
the train to meet
could this be she asked
the ladys husband
pulling me out of his
coat pocket by the neck and

holding me up with a
dazed expression on his face
it could not said his
wife with a look of
scorn . . .
         archy

              don marquis

Two's Company

(The sad story of the man who didn't believe in ghosts.)

They said the house was haunted, but
He laughed at them and said, 'Tut, tut!
I've never heard such tittle-tattle
As ghosts that groan and chains that rattle;
And just to prove I'm in the right,
Please leave me here to spend the night.'
They winked absurdly, tried to smother
Their ignorant laughter, nudged each other,
And left him just as dusk was falling
With a hunchback moon and screech-owls
    calling –
Not that this troubled him one bit;
In fact, he was quite glad of it,
Knowing it's every sane man's mission
To contradict all superstition.

But what is that? Outside it seemed
As if chains rattled, someone screamed!
Come come, its merely nerves, he's certain
(But just the same, he draws the curtain).
The stroke of twelve – but there's no clock!
He shuts the door and turns the lock.
(Of course, he knows that no one's there,
But no harm's done by taking care!);
Someone's outside – the silly joker,
(He may as well pick up the poker!)
That noise again! He checks the doors,
Shutters the windows, makes a pause
To seek the safest place to hide –
(The cupboard's strong – he creeps inside).

'Not that there's anything to fear,'
He tells himself, when at his ear
A voice breathes softly, 'How do you do!
I am the ghost. Pray, who are you?'

Raymond Wilson

Sheer Nonsense

No Knees and No Nose

The rain has no knees
The snow has no nose
And so I suppose
The rain cannot graze
Its nothings of knees
And the snow when it froze
Couldn't sniff with a nose
All the smells that arose
From a pigsty or rose
And nobody sees
The noseless snow freeze
On shivery days
And nobody knows
How the rain ever goes
Soaking everyone's toes
Without walking with knees
But falls through the trees
Out of thundery skies
And falls on the seas
Without knowing the size
Of the squashy wet shoes
It would have if its toes
Were attached to some knees
And when the rain freezes

The snow which it causes
Has no knees *and* no nose
Because of the laws
That everyone knows
Which say 'Rain has no knees'
And 'Snow has no nose'.
But do you suppose
The rain cares about those
Laws with their clauses
Concerning no knees,
Or the snow ever pays
Attention to pleas
From a pig or a rose
For a nice snowy nose?
No, never. A sneeze
Wouldn't help when it snows
And as far as no knees goes
The rain goes its way
Wherever it pleases
Untroubled by kneeses.

So there's no special cause
To make new decrees
To alter the laws
That the rain has no knees
And the snow has no nose.

Anthony Thwaite

Scorflufus

There are many diseases,
That strike people's kneeses,
Scorflufus! is one by name
It comes from the East
Packed in bladders of yeast
So the Chinese must take half the blame.

There's a case in the files
Of Sir Barrington-Pyles
While hunting a fox one day
Shot up in the air
And *remained hanging there!*
While the hairs on his socks turned grey!

Aye! Scorflufus had struck!
At man, beast and duck.
And the knees of the world went Bong!
Some knees went Ping!
Other knees turned to string
From Balham to old Hong-Kong.

Should you hold your life dear,
Then the remedy's clear,
If you're offered some yeast – don't eat it!
Turn the offer down flat –
Don your travelling hat –
Put an egg in your boot – and beat it!

Spike Milligan

Advice to a Cannibal

(from a suggestion by Lewis Carroll)

Never stew your sister
You'll be sorry when you've missed her,
For there's no fun in cooking
Anyone who is looking
Something like yourself.

Never bake your brother
He's so much like your mother
And they'll both be very bitter
If you eat him in a fritter
At a midnight barbecue.

Never fry your father –
There'd be a great palaver,
And he'd come and haunt you nightly
And bring you indigestion
Like an undigested question.

Never grill your grandad,
Although he was a bad lad,
You'll need a steady nerve
To pepper, salt and serve
Your chief and royal ancestor.

Whatever's on the menu,
Make sure it's never *you*.
Try to stay uneaten,
And avoid becoming beaten
In an omelette or soufflé.

Kenneth Agar

I Sat Belonely Down a Tree

I sat belonely down a tree,
humbled fat and small.
A little lady sing to me
I couldn't see at all.

I'm looking up and at the sky,
To find such wondrous voice.
Puzzly, puzzle, wonder why,
I hear but have no choice.

'Speak up, come forth, you ravel me,'
I potty menthol shout.
'I know you hiddy by this tree.'
But still she won't come out.

Such softly singing lulled me sleep,
an hour or two or so,
I wakeny slow and took a peep
and still no lady show.

Then suddy on a little twig
I thought I see a sight,
A tiny little tiny pig,
that sing with all its might.

'I thought you were a lady.'
I giggle – well I may,
To my surprise the lady,
got up – and flew away.

John Lennon

Maveric

Maveric Prowles
Had Rumbling Bowles
That thundered in the night
It shook the bedrooms all around
And gave the folks a fright.

The doctor called;
He was appalled
When through his stethoscope
He heard the sound of a baying hound,
And the acrid smell of smoke.

Was there a cure?
'The higher the fewer,'
The learned doctor said,
Then turned poor Maveric inside out
And stood him on his head.

'Just as I thought,
You've been and caught
An Asiatic flue –
You mustn't go near dogs I fear
Unless they come near you.'

Poor Maveric cried.
He went cross-eyed,
His legs went green and blue.
The doctor hit him with a club
And charged him one and two.

And so my friend
This is the end,
A warning to the few:
Stay clear of doctors to the end
Or they'll get rid of you.

Spike Milligan

The Computer's First Christmas Card

jollymerry
hollyberry
jollyberry
merryholly
happyjolly
jollyjelly
jellybelly
bellymerry
hollyheppy
jollyMolly
marryJerry
merryHarry
hoppyBarry
heppyJarry
boppyheppy
berryjorry
jorryjolly
moppyjelly
Mollymerry
Jerryjolly
bellyboppy
jorryhoppy
hollymoppy

Barrymerry
Jarryhappy
happyboppy
boppyjolly
jollymerry
merrymerry
merrymerry
merryChris
ammerryasa
Chrismerry
aSMERRYCHR
YSANTHEMUM

Edwin Morgan

Some Odds and Ends to End With

A Wessex Prayer

God bless me and me wife,
Me son John and his wife,
  Us four;
  No more!

Anon.

Would You Believe It?

A daring young lady of Guam
Observed, 'The Pacific's so calm
  I'll swim out for a lark.'
  She met a large shark . . .
Let us now sing the Ninetieth Psalm.

Anon.

A rocket explorer named Wright
Once travelled much faster than light.
   He set out one day
   In a relative way,
And returned on the previous night.

Anon.

A glutton who came from the Rhine
Was asked at what hour he'd dine.
　　He replied, 'At eleven,
　　　At three, five, and seven,
And eight and a quarter to nine.'

　　　　　　　　Anon.

Of a sudden the great prima donna
Cried, 'Gawd, but my voice is a goner!'
   But a cat in the wings
    Said, 'I know how she sings,'
And finished the solo with honour.

Anon.

There was an old woman of Harrow
Who visited in a wheelbarrow,
And her servant before
Knock'd loud at each door
To announce the old woman of Harrow

Anon.

There was a young lady of Riga
Who rode with a smile on a tiger;
  They returned from this ride
  With the lady inside,
And the smile on the face of the tiger.

                  Anon.

Boniface

Old Boniface he loved good cheer,
   And took his glass of Burton,
And when the nights grew sultry hot
   He slept without a shirt on.

Anon.

The Answers

'When did the world begin and how?'
I asked a lamb, a goat, a cow:

'What's it all about and why?'
I asked a hog as he went by:

'Where will the whole thing end, and when?'
I asked a duck, a goose, a hen:

And I copied all the answers too,
A quack, a honk, an oink, a moo.

Robert Clairmont

Index of Authors

Index of First Lines

Acknowledgements

For permission to use copyright material the editor and publishers are indebted to the following:

Angus & Robertson U.K. Ltd. for 'The Magic Pudding' by Norman Lindsay from 'First Slice', *The Magic Pudding*; Jonathan Cape Ltd. for 'I sat Belonely Down a Tree' by John Lennon from *In His Own Write* and 'The National Health Cow' by John Lennon from *A Spaniard in the Works*; Dennis Dobson (Dobson Books) Ltd. for 'Maveric' by Spike Milligan from *Silly Verse for Kids* and 'Scorflufus' by Spike Milligan from *A Dustbin of Milligan*; Faber & Faber Ltd. for 'Crocodile' by Kornei Chukousky translated by Richard Coe from *Crocodile*, 'Pussy Café' by Don Marquis from *Archy's Life of Mehitabel*, 'The Kitty-Cat Bird', 'The Lady and the Bear' and 'The Serpent' by Theodore Roethke from his *Collected Poems*; J. A. Lindon for his poem 'A Cautionary Tale' from *Yet More Comic & Curious Verse*; London Magazine for 'The Computer's First Christmas Card' by Edwin Morgan; George Macbeth for his poem 'The Red Herring' from *A Doomsday Book*; Macmillan & Co. Ltd., London & Basingstoke for 'No Knees and No Nose' by Anthony Thwaite from *Allsorts 2* and 'Two's Company' by Raymond Wilson

89

More Zebra poetry books

Nothing Serious

Poems selected by Kenneth Agar

A companion volume to *Nothing Solemn*, this anthology of humorous verse offers fun and laughter to readers of all ages.

Come Follow Me

Poems for the very young

A lively and interesting collection of poems for young children which has already delighted thousands of readers all over the world.

The Swinging Rainbow

Happy Landings

selected by Howard Sergeant

Two collections of old favourites and modern poems, specially chosen to appeal to young people. They are anthologies to be read and enjoyed again and again and there is something in them for everyone.

Out of School

compiled by Dennis Saunders

What do you do when away from school? Climb trees, play games, go skating, go fishing ...? There are many things to do in your leisure time and these poems are all about them.

Books of Hobbies

The Zebra Indoor Book

by Rita Davies

Filled with an abundance of ideas for things to collect and make.

The Zebra Outdoor Book

by Frederick Wilkinson

Full of ideas that will start an absorbing hobby or fill a free afternoon.

Make your own Collection

by Joyce and Cyril Parsons

All kinds of suggestions for preparing, arranging, displaying and adding to specimens so that an accumulation of objects becomes a real collection.

Do you like craftwork?

The Zebra Book of Papercraft

by G. Roland Smith

A hundred different models, all made with paper and without a knife; they all take very little time and can often be joined together if you want to build up a really impressive construction.

Models from Junk

Junk on the Move

by Brenda B. Jackson

With the help of the simple instructions in these books many models and creatures can be created out of the bits and pieces to be found in every home.

What do you know?

Ask me a question

by J. Perry Harvey

All knowledge is exciting and it is quite remarkable how much you can learn without even thinking about it. You can have a lot of fun, too, from the many and varied quizzes which make up *Ask me a question*. They lead on to all kinds of interesting points of discovery and, at the same time, provide hours of amusement.

Give Me the Answer

by J. Perry Harvey

J. Perry Harvey's second Zebra quiz book is packed with quizzes and puzzles on a wide variety of subjects, and will not only test just how much you do know, but will also give you the chance to find out about many subjects that are new to you.